PIANO • VOCAL

BROADWAY MUSICALS
Show by Show
1989-2005

T0081472

CONTENTS

ISBN 1-4234-0866-7

HAL•LEONARD®
CORPORATION

7777 W. BLUEMOUND RD. P.O. BOX 13819 MILWAUKEE, WI 53213

Visit Hal Leonard Online at
www.halleonard.com

BROADWAY MUSICALS
Show by Show
1989-2005

CONTENTS
Chronological by Show

GRAND HOTEL

Music and Lyrics:
Robert Wright, George Forrest

Additional Music and Lyrics:
Maury Yeston

Book:
Luther Davis,
based on the novel by Vicki Baum

Producers:
Martin Richards, Mary Lea Johnson,
Sam Crothers, etc.

Director and Choreographer:
Tommy Tune

Cast:
Karen Akers, David Carroll, Timothy Jerome,
Michael Jeter, Jane Krakowski,
Liliane Montevecchi, John Wylie

Songs:
Grand Parade
As It Should Be
At the Grand Hotel
The Grand Tango (Table with a View)
Maybe My Baby Loves Me
Villa on a Hill
I Want to Go to Hollywood
Love Can't Happen
What You Need
Bonjour Amour
The Grand Charleston (H-A-P-P-Y)
We'll Take a Glass Together
I Waltz Alone
Roses at the Station

New York Run:
Martin Beck Theatre;
George Gershwin Theatre,
November 12, 1989;
1017 p.

*B*ased on a novel by Vicki Baum, *Grand Hotel* interweaves the staff and guests at a posh Berlin hotel *c*1930, just as the star-studded film of 1932 mixed the stories of Greta Garbo, Lionel Barrymore, Joan Crawford and a host of others. On Broadway, the stories included the penniless Baron's plans to steal the aging ballerina's jewels (he instead falls in love with her), the businessman who wrestles with his conscience, an aspiring actress who reluctantly peddles her flesh and the accountant with a zeal for living in the face of a fatal disease. The sub-plots intermingled and intersected predominantly through dance in the Tommy Tune production. Aspiring actress, but current typist, Flaemmchen confides to the girl in the mirror, "I Want to Go to Hollywood."

ASPECTS OF LOVE

Music:
Andrew Lloyd Webber

Lyrics:
Don Black, Charles Hart

Book:
Andrew Lloyd Webber,
based on the novel by David Garnett

Producer:
The Really Useful Theatre Company Ltd.

Director:
Trevor Nunn

Choreographer:
Gillian Lynne

Cast:
Michael Ball, Suzanne Briar, Walter Charles,
Kevin Colson, Ann Crumb,
Deanna and Danielle Du Clos,
Don Goodspeed, Kathleen Rowe McAllen

Songs:
Love Changes Everything
Parlez-Vous Français?
Seeing Is Believing
Chanson d'enfance
She'd Be Far Better Off with You
Other Pleasures
There Is More to Love
Mermaid Song
The First Man You Remember
Hand Me the Wine and the Dice
Anything but Lonely

New York Run:
Broadhurst Theatre, April 8, 1990;
377 p.

*A*spects of Love is based on an autobiographical novel by David Garnett, a nephew of Virginia Woolf. The show had an intimate production style, with orchestrations that threw out the brass in favor of a chamber music sound. It follows a group of characters over nearly two decades of interweaving relationships. The story begins with a 17-year-old boy, Alex, who is infatuated with an actress, Rose, in her mid-20s. The actress eventually has a love affair with Alex's uncle, and they marry. Along the way almost everyone winds up in love with, or broken-hearted by, all the others. The plot is emotionally complex, as are the characters and their relationships. An anthem of love's force in our world, "Love Changes Everything" is sung by Alex to open and close the first act, as well as to end the show.

MISS SAIGON

Music:
Claude-Michel Schönberg

Lyrics:
Alain Boublil, Richard Maltby, Jr.

Book:
Alain Boublil, Claude-Michel Schönberg

Producer:
Cameron Mackintosh

Director:
Nicholas Hytner

Choreographer:
Bob Avian

Cast:
Hinton Battle, Barry K. Bernal, Liz Callaway,
Kam Cheng, Willy Falk,
Jonathan Pryce, Lea Salonga

Songs:
The Heat Is On in Saigon
The Movie in My Mind
Why God Why?
Sun and Moon
The Last Night of the World
I Still Believe
If You Want to Die in Bed
I'd Give My Life for You
Bui-Doi
The American Dream

New York Run:
Broadway Theatre, April 11, 1991;
4092 p.

*A*s follow-up to their hit *Les Misérables*, Boublil and Schönberg boldly chose to update and transpose the Belasco/Puccini tale of the tragic Madame Butterfly to the Vietnam War of the 1970s. Instead of a sailor in 19th century Japan, the story now deals with a Marine living through the fall of Saigon at the end of the war. As in the original story, there is a hot romance between the soldier and a native girl, maybe even love, but then the lovers are torn apart by history. *Miss Saigon* follows the soldier (Chris) as he attempts to build a civilian life back home—with an American wife. Meanwhile, the girl, Kim, is left to raise their half-American child in Communist Vietnam, all the while plotting to escape and rejoin her man, whom she assumes is waiting for her. The writers cite a news photograph of a woman giving up her child to an American G.I. as the genesis of the idea. The production is noted for a life-size helicopter that descends on the stage and whisks Chris, but not Kim, away as the enemy conquers the city. "I'd Give My Life for You" is Kim's desperate lullabye to her baby.

BEAUTY AND THE BEAST

Music:
Alan Menken

Lyrics:
Howard Ashman, Tim Rice

Book:
Linda Woolverton

Producer:
Walt Disney Productions

Director:
Robert Jess Roth

Choreographer:
Matt West

Cast:
Gary Beach, Tom Bosley, Susan Egan,
Beth Fowler, Heath Lamberts, Terrence Mann,
Burke Moses, Brian Press, Kenny Raskin

Songs:
Belle
No Matter What
Me
Home
Gaston
How Long Must This Go On?
Be Our Guest
If I Can't Love Her
Something There
Human Again
Beauty and the Beast

New York Run:
Palace Theatre;
Lunt-Fontanne Theatre,
April 18, 1994;
still running April, 2006

*D*isney made its Broadway debut with a big-budget adaptation of its own 1991 Oscar-nominated animated film musical. Like the classic fairy tale on which it is based, *Beauty and the Beast* tells the story of a witch who transforms a haughty prince into a fearsome Beast (and his retainers into household objects). Her spell can be broken only when the prince learns how to love, and how to inspire love. Lyricist Ashman died in 1991 before the film opened. The stage score includes several trunk songs written for the film, but not used, plus five new songs with lyrics by Broadway veteran Rice. Belle is a dreamy, bookish ingenue, a bit of a social outcast in her own way. Much to her surprise she falls in love with the initially brutish Beast. "Beauty and the Beast" is sung by Mrs. Potts as a backdrop to the romantic dinner between the Beast and Belle.

SUNSET BOULEVARD

Music:
Andrew Lloyd Webber

Lyrics:
Don Black, Christopher Hampton

Book:
Don Black, Christopher Hampton,
based on the film by Billy Wilder

Producer:
The Really Useful Theatre Company Ltd.

Director:
Trevor Nunn

Choreographer:
Bob Avian

Cast:
Alan Campbell, Glenn Close, George Hearn,
Alice Ripley, Alan Oppenheimer,
Vincent Tumeo

Songs:
Let's Have Lunch
Surrender
With One Look
The Greatest Star of All
Every Movie's a Circus
Girl Meets Boy
New Ways to Dream
The Perfect Year
This Time Next Year
Sunset Boulevard
As If We Never Said Goodbye
Too Much in Love to Care

New York Run:
Minskoff Theatre, November 17, 1994;
977 p.

*B*ased on the 1950 Billy Wilder film, *Sunset Boulevard* provided Broadway and the West End with one of the great diva vehicles ever. Dealing with a tortured woman whose advancing age leads to rejection and madness, this musical shows the degenerate aftereffects of Hollywood stardom in all their gothic glory. The show premiered in London in 1993 with Patti LuPone as the former silent screen star Norma Desmond who is desperate to make a comeback (though she loathes that word). After several lawsuits, the Broadway role went to Glenn Close, who had played the role in Los Angeles. The story involves handsome young screenwriter Joe Gillis who stumbles into Norma Desmond's life. She falls in love with him, and he accepts her lavish attention. Miss Desmond has a pathetic plan to return to the screen with her own hopelessly-overwritten adaptation of *Salome*. She thrills when the studio requests a meeting. But she's then crushed when she learns they don't want her—they want her vintage car, as an antique prop. Her life and sanity quickly fly apart, with tragic consequences for all. The score includes two juicy, pull-out-the-stops soliloquies for Norma. In "With One Look," she tells Joe about the magical power she had over audiences.

VICTOR/VICTORIA

Music:
Henry Mancini

Additional Music:
Frank Wildhorn

Lyrics:
Leslie Bricusse

Book:
Blake Edwards

Producers:
Blake Edwards, Tony Adams, John Scher, etc.

Director:
Blake Edwards

Choreographer:
Rob Marshall

Cast:
Julie Andrews, Michael Cripe, Adam Heller,
Gregory Jbara, Michael Nouri, Tony Roberts,
Robert B. Shull, Rachel York

Songs:
Paris by Night
If I Were a Man
Trust Me
Le Jazz Hot!
Paris Makes Me Horny
Crazy World
King's Dilemma
You and Me
Almost a Love Song
Chicago, Illinois
Living in the Shadows
Victor/Victoria

New York Run:
Marquis Theatre, October 25, 1995;
734 p.

*A*fter a 35-year absence, Julie Andrews made her ballyhooed return to Broadway in this stage adaptation of her 1982 film musical, directed and co-written by her husband, Blake Edwards. Desperate for a job in Depression-era Paris, singer Victoria (Andrews) turns to her friend, the aging self-described "drag queen" Toddy. He convinces Victoria to pose as a female impersonator named Victor – making her a woman pretending to be a man pretending to be a woman. (S)he's a smash, and attracts the attentions of King Marchan, a Chicago gangster who feels strangely attracted to "Victor." Despite the apparent awkwardness and obstacles, their love blossoms. "Living in the Shadows" reveals that Victoria no longer wants to be a man.

RENT

Music and Lyrics:
Jonathan Larson

Book:
Jonathan Larson

Producers:
Jeffrey Seller, Kevin McCollum,
Allan S. Gordon, New York Theatre Workshop

Director:
Michael Greif

Choreographer:
Marlies Yearby

Cast:
Taye Diggs, Wilson Jermaine Heredia,
Jesse L. Martin, Idina Menzel, Adam Pascal,
Anthony Rapp, Daphne Rubin-Vega,
Fredi Walker

Songs:
Rent
One Song Glory
Out Tonight
Another Day
Santa Fe
I'll Cover You
Seasons of Love
Take Me or Leave Me
Without You
Halloween
What You Own
Your Eyes

New York Run:
Nederlander Theatre, April 29, 1996;
still running April, 2006

*O*ne of the emblematic Broadway shows of the 1990s, Jonathan Larson's alternative-rock musical relocates the story of opera's *La Boheme* to the '90s in New York's Bohemian East Village. Instead of dying of consumption, the central character, also named Mimi, is dying of AIDS. The characters are a mix of various types of contemporary artists: a filmmaker, an HIV-positive musician, a drug-addicted dancer, a drag queen. Despite struggles, the friends remain devoted to one another. The compelling alternative-rock score has a gritty realism that had special appeal for young theatregoers. A parable of hope, love and loyalty, *Rent* received great acclaim, winning the Pulitzer Prize for Drama, a Tony® Award for Best Musical, and many other awards. It quickly transferred from Off-Broadway's New York Theatre Workshop to a Broadway theatre that was redesigned especially for the show, to capture its East Village atmosphere. Bound up with the show's message of the preciousness of life is the tragic real-life story of its composer/librettist Jonathan Larson, who died suddenly the night of the final dress rehearsal before the first Off-Broadway performance. "Seasons of Love" begins Act II. In the aftermath of the Act I riot, the onstage community poses the question, "How do you measure the life of a woman or a man?"

JEKYLL & HYDE

Music:
Frank Wildhorn

Lyrics:
Leslie Bricusse

Book:
Leslie Bricusse

Producers:
PACE Theatrical Group, Inc., Fox Theatricals

Director:
Robin Phillips

Choreographer:
Joey Pizzi

Cast:
Robert Cuccioli, Linda Eder, Barrie Ingham,
George Merritt, Christine Noll

Songs:
Lost in the Darkness
Façade
Take Me as I Am
No One Knows Who I Am
Good and Evil
This Is the Moment
Alive!
Sympathy, Tenderness
Someone Like You
Murder, Murder!
Once upon a Dream
In His Eyes
It's a Dangerous Game
A New Life
Confrontation

New York Run:
Plymouth Theatre, April 28, 1997;
1543 p.

*B*ased on Robert Louis Stevenson's 1886 novella *Dr. Jekyll and Mr. Hyde*, this show took nearly a decade to arrive on Broadway. However, the first full score by pop composer Frank Wildhorn was already familiar to many lovers of musical theatre from two widely circulated concept albums. A North American tour also helped the show's momentum before Broadway. As in the Stevenson book, a well-meaning scientist, Dr. Henry Jekyll, invents a potion that separates the noble side of man's nature from the evil, bestial side. "This Is the Moment," sings Jekyll exultantly, as he resolves to test the new potion on himself. But, as his own guinea pig, Jekyll soon finds he has unleashed an uncontrollable monster, Mr. Hyde, who cuts a murderous swath through London.

TITANIC

Music and Lyrics:
Maury Yeston

Story and Book:
Peter Stone

Producers:
Dodger Endemol Theatricals,
Richard S. Pechter,
The John F. Kennedy Center for the
Performing Arts

Director:
Richard Jones

Choreographer:
Lynne Taylor-Corbett

Cast:
Michael Cerveris, Victoria Clark,
John Cunningham, David Garrison,
Brian D'Arcy James, Jennifer Piech

Songs:
How Did They Build Titanic?
There She Is
I Must Get on That Ship
Godspeed Titanic (Sail On)
Barrett's Song
What a Remarkable Age
To Be a Captain
Lady's Maid
The Proposal
The Night Was Alive
No Moon
Autumn
We'll Meet Tomorrow
Still

New York Run:
Lunt-Fontanne Theatre, April 23, 1997;
804 p.

*T*he whole idea of a musical about the sinking of the luxury liner *Titanic* was unsettling to many Broadwayites. Few thought Yeston, Stone and company could pull it off. And reports of technological glitches during the early previews threatened to turn the whole project into a joke. And yet, when they finished counting the Tony® ballots in 1997, *Titanic* won for Best Musical. Credit the strength of Yeston's score that explored the emotional nuances of a whole tapestry of characters and situations. The music takes theatregoers inside the head of the captain, the shipbuilder, the millionaires, the social climbers and the illiterate immigrants, each with their dreams and worries that are changed forever by the events of that fateful journey. "Godspeed Titanic" is the prayerful farewell sung by the company as the fully-boarded ship begins her first and final voyage.

SIDE SHOW

Music:
Henry Krieger

Lyrics and Book:
Bill Russell

Producers:
Emanuel Azenberg, Joseph Nederlander,
Herschel Waxman, Janice McKenna,
Scott Nederlander

Director and Choreographer:
Robert Longbottom

Cast:
Ken Jennings, Norm Lewis, Jeff McCarthy,
Hugh Panaro, Alice Ripley, Emily Skinner

Songs:
Come Look at the Freaks
Happy Birthday to You and You
Like Everyone Else
The Devil You Know
Feelings You've Got to Hide
When I'm by Your Side
Say Goodbye to the Freak Show
Leave Me Alone
We Share Everything
Who Will Love Me as I Am?
Private Conversation
One Plus One Equals Three
You Should Be Loved
Tunnel of Love
I Will Never Leave You

New York Run:
Richard Rodgers Theatre, October 16, 1997;
91 p.

*S*he's Daisy; she's Violet. They're Siamese twins. That's the offbeat story of this fictionalized biography of real-life joined-at-the-hip twins Daisy and Violet Hilton, who climbed from carnival freak show through vaudeville to the Ziegfeld Follies in the early decades of the 20th century. The musical concentrates on their doomed romance with the two men who act as their coach and agent, but who ultimately can't get over what they see as the sisters' deformity. The show attracted a small but devoted cult that was unable to keep the show running more than three months. Stars Emily Skinner and Alice Ripley, who suggested their conjoined state simply by standing side by side and pressing together one hip each, have appeared together repeatedly since, including James Joyce's *The Dead* (2000). The composer of *Dreamgirls* supplied the sisters with another powerhouse Act I finale, "Who Will Love Me as I Am?" which recalls his "And I Am Telling You I'm Not Going."

THE LION KING

Music:
Elton John

Lyrics:
Tim Rice

Additional Music and Lyrics:
Lebo M, Mark Mancina, Jay Rifkin,
Julie Taymor, Hans Zimmer

Book:
Roger Allers, Irene Mecchi,
adapted from the screenplay by Irene Mecchi,
Jonathan Roberts, Linda Woolverton

Producer:
Disney Theatrical Productions

Director:
Julie Taymor

Choreographer:
Garth Fagan

Cast:
Gina Breedlove, Kevin Cahoon, Max Casella,
Tracy Nicole Chapman, Heather Headley,
Geoff Hoyle, Scott Irby-Ranniar,
Tsidii Le Loka, Stanley Wayne Mathis,
Jason Raize, Tom Alan Robbins,
Kajuana Shuford, John Vickery,
Samuel E. Wright

Songs:
Circle of Life
The Morning Report
I Just Can't Wait to Be King
Chow Down
They Live in You
Be Prepared
Hakuna Matata
The Madness of King Scar
Shadowland
Endless Night
Can You Feel the Love Tonight
He Lives in You (Reprise)

New York Run:
New Amsterdam Theatre,
November 13, 1997;
still running April, 2006

A fantastic triumph of art design and choreography, Julie Taymor's adaptation to the stage of the 1994 Disney movie won both critical and popular praise. Lavish sets and costumes, including actors on stilts, set this production high above other movie-to-stage adaptations. The Broadway score incorporates all the music from the original movie, along with new material. Mufasa, king of the lions, is murdered by his brother Scar. Young Simba is led to believe he killed his father and runs away to exile. As an adult, Simba returns to overthrow the evil Scar and claim his birthright as king. Early in the show, Mufasa instructs Simba to avoid the territory of the hyenas, but the brash young cub deliberately disobeys. He, along with the lioness cub Nala, only narrowly avoid becoming hyena chow when Mufasa comes to their rescue. In "They Live in You," Mufasa reminds his son of the great responsibilities that await him once he becomes king.

AIDA

Music:
Elton John

Lyrics:
Tim Rice

Book:
Linda Woolverton, Robert Falls,
David Henry Hwang,
based on the opera by Giuseppe Verdi

Producer:
Hyperion Theatricals

Director:
Robert Falls

Choreographer:
Wayne Cilento

Cast:
Tyrees Allen, Heather Headley, John Hickok,
Daniel Oreskes, Adam Pascal,
Damian Perkins, Sherie Rene Scott

Songs:
Every Story Is a Love Story
Fortune Favors the Brave
The Past Is Another Land
Another Pyramid
How I Know You
My Strongest Suit
Enchantment Passing Through
Dance of the Robe
Not Me
Elaborate Lives
The Gods Love Nubia
A Step Too Far
Easy as Life
Like Father Like Son
Radames' Letter
Written in the Stars
I Know the Truth

New York Run:
Palace Theatre, March 23, 2000;
1852 p.

*A*ida is based on the 1871 opera by Giuseppe Verdi (libretto by Antonio Ghislanzoni) about an Ethiopian princess who is captured during wartime by the enemy Egyptians. Radames, an Egyptian general, and Aida fall in love. Aida is the object of scorn by the Egyptian king's daughter, Amneris, who is also in love with Radames. Radames first professes his love for Aida in "Elaborate Lives," where they decide that circumstances can no longer keep them apart. Much later, Radames plans to call off his wedding to Amneris, but Aida convinces him to keep up appearances so she can flee from captivity with her father. At their parting, they wonder if their love was doomed at the outset. The story ends tragically with the death of the two lovers.

THE FULL MONTY

Music and Lyrics:
David Yazbek

Book:
Terrence McNally

Producers:
Fox Searchlight Pictures, Lindsay Law,
Thomas Hall

Director:
Jack O'Brien

Choreographer:
Jerry Mitchell

Cast:
John Ellison Conlee, Nicholas Cutro,
Jason Danieley, Lisa Datz,
Andre De Shields, Jay Douglas,
Laura Marie Duncan, Angelo Fraboni,
Thomas Michael Fiss, Kathleen Freeman

Songs:
Scrap
It's a Woman's World
Man
Big-Ass Rock
Life with Harold
Big Black Man
You Rule My World
Michael Jordan's Ball
Jeanette's Showbiz Number
Breeze Off the River
The Goods
You Walk with Me
Let It Go

New York Run:
Eugene O'Neill Theatre, October 26, 2000;
770 p.

*B*ased on the successful British movie of the same name, *The Full Monty* is David Yazbek's first foray into Broadway. The scene for the stage musical is changed to Buffalo, New York. The men in the story are unemployed factory workers. Determined to support themselves and families, the decidedly-average group form a Chippendale's type strip act, baring everything (as the British phrase "the full monty" implies) for entertainment. Each of the guys has a personal obstacle to overcome, and the act of baring it publicly is a symbol of personal freedom. Late in the show, with the rest of the guys already onstage for the big finish, Jerry hangs back, afraid of failure yet again. His son, Nathan confronts him and tells him straight out: "This time, don't be what everyone thinks you are—a loser." Jerry finally understands he has an opportunity to show the people who love him that he *can* follow through and not be afraid of dreams and responsibilities. He understands that *The Full Monty* isn't just about showing off the outside, it's about what all of us have on the inside. One only has to "Let It Go."

THE PRODUCERS

Music and Lyrics:
Mel Brooks

Book:
Mel Brooks, Thomas Meechan

Producers:
Rocco Landesman, SFX Theatrical Group, etc.

Director and Choreographer:
Susan Stroman

Cast:
Roger Bart, Gary Beach, Matthew Broderick,
Madeleine Doherty, Kathy Fitzgerald,
Eric Gunhus, Cady Huffman,
Nathan Lane, Peter Marinos,
Brad Oscar, Jennifer Smith, Ray Wills

Songs:
Opening Night
The King of Broadway
We Can Do It
I Wanna Be a Producer
In Old Bavaria
Der Guten Tag Hop-Clop
Keep It Gay
When You Got It, Flaunt It
Along Came Bialy
That Face
Haben Sie gehört das Deutsche Band?
You Never Say Good Luck on Opening Night
Springtime for Hitler
Where Did We Go Right?
Betrayed
'Til Him
Prisoners of Love

New York Run:
St. James Theatre, April 19, 2001;
still running April, 2006

*M*el Brooks swept critics and audiences off their feet in New York with this show, adapted from his 1968 movie *The Producers*. A couple of songs from the movie were incorporated into the otherwise new stage score. The story concerns washed-up Broadway producer Max Bialystock and his nerdy accountant Leo Bloom, who has dreams of being a producer himself. During an audit of Max's books, Leo offhandedly remarks that one could make more money producing a flop than a hit. That flop is *Springtime for Hitler*, penned by nutcase Nazi-sympathizer Franz Liebkind. Max and Leo visit him to get the rights, while Franz sings of the beauty "In Old Bavaria" on the roof, accompanied by his pigeons. The two eventually produce the show, financed by Max's wooing of countless rich old ladies ("Along Came Bialy"). Once the show is a go, the producers look for the worst cast ever, and in a surprisingly "good" performance, Liebkind wins the role of Adolph Hitler through his audition song "Haben Sie Gehört Das Deutsche Band?" The show is a surprise hit, the title song a showstopper, and Bialystock and Bloom are in trouble. All ends well, after a brief prison detour. The original cast included Broadway stars Nathan Lane (Max) and Matthew Broderick (Leo). The director and most of the lead actors from Broadway were in the 2005 movie musical.

URINETOWN

Music:
Mark Hollman

Lyrics:
Mark Hollman, Greg Kotis

Book:
Greg Kotis

Producers:
The Araca Group, Dodger Theatricals

Director:
John Rando

Choreographer:
John Carrafa

Cast:
David Beach, Jennifer Cody, Rachel Coloff,
Rick Crom, John Cullum, John Deyle,
Hunter Foster, Victor W. Hawks,
Ken Jennings, Spencer Kayden

Songs:
Too Much Exposition
Urinetown
It's a Privilege to Pee
Mr. Cladwell
Follow Your Heart
Look at the Sky
Don't Be the Bunny
What Is Urinetown?
Run, Freedom, Run!
Why Did I Listen to That Man?
Tell Her I Love Her
We're Not Sorry
I See a River

New York Run:
Henry Miller's Theatre, September 20, 2001;
965 p.

*W*ithout seeing the show, it is hard to believe a production called *Urinetown* would come to Broadway, but it did, and had a successful run at that. Greg Kotis had the seed of the idea while broke in Europe and faced with a Parisian pay-per-use toilet. This helped him envision the drought stricken world where a greedy conglomerate, Urine Good Company, owns all the toilets in the city, thus making it a "Privilege to Pee." This show delights in its self-awareness and lambasting of the musical genre, with intentionally cheesy lyrics and a wee plot. Bobby Strong helps the masses to overthrow the corrupt company, while falling for the boss's daughter, Hope. She gives him advice, after the jailing of his own father Old Man Strong, to "Follow Your Heart." The show's original opening date of September 13, 2001, was postponed due to the World Trade Center attacks.

MAMMA MIA!

Music and Lyrics:
Benny Andersson, Björn Ulvaeus

Book:
Catherine Johnson

Producers:
Judy Craymer, Richard East, Björn Ulvaeus,
Littlestar Ltd.

Director:
Phyllida Lloyd

Choreographer:
Anthony Van Laast

Cast:
Tonya Doran, Sara Inbar, Judy Kaye,
David Keeley, Joe Machota, Tina Maddigan,
Ken Marks, Karen Mason, Dean Nolen,
Louise Pitre, Mark Price,
Michael B. Washington

Songs:
Honey, Honey
Money, Money, Money
Thank You for the Music

Mamma Mia
Chiquitita
Dancing Queen
Lay All Your Love on Me
Super Trouper
Gimme! Gimme! Gimme!
The Name of the Game
Voulez Vous
Under Attack
One of Us
S.O.S.
Does Your Mother Know
Knowing Me, Knowing You
Our Last Summer
Slipping through My Fingers
Winner Takes It All
Take a Chance on Me
I Do I Do I Do I Do I Do
I Have a Dream

New York Run:
Winter Garden Theatre,
Cadillac Winter Garden Theatre,
October 18, 2001;
still running April, 2006

*M*amma Mia! is a "jukebox musical" culled from the catalogue of Swedish pop group ABBA. Over 20 songs are used in the show, more or less in their original form, with a new book created for the stage production. The ads for the musical capsulize the plot: "A mother. A daughter. Three possible dads. And a trip down the aisle you'll never forget." It all takes place on a small Greek Island on the day of the daughter's wedding. The daughter in question, Sophie, has invited all three possible dads to the wedding. Her mother, Donna, who has been kept in the dark about the additional guests, is somewhat shocked when all three former beaus arrive on the wedding day ("Mamma Mia"). She escapes to her room. Rosie and Tanya, former bandmates of hers from a chick group, follow her there and try to cheer her up. In the process, they discover mementos of their former rock band days and try to see if they've still got it ("Dancing Queen"). This good time for audiences has found success in London, Broadway, a North American tour, a standing show in Las Vegas, and performances in countries as diverse as South Africa, Sweden and Korea.

THOROUGHLY MODERN MILLIE

New Music:
Jeanine Tesori

New Lyrics:
Dick Scanlan

Book:
Dick Scanlan, Richard Morris

Producers:
Michael Leavitt, Fox Theatricals, Hal Luftig,
Stewart F. Lane, James L. Nederlander, etc.

Director:
Michael Mayer

Choreographer:
Rob Ashford

Cast:
Gavin Creel, Angela Christian, Sutton Foster,
Harriet Harris, Marc Kudisch

Songs:
Not for the Life of Me
Thoroughly Modern Millie
How the Other Half Lives
The Speed Test
They Don't Know
What Do I Need with Love?
Only in New York
Jimmy
Forget about the Boy
Ah! Sweet Mystery of Life
I'm Falling in Love with Someone
I Turned the Corner
Long as I'm Here with You
Gimme Gimme

New York Run:
Marquis Theatre, April 18, 2002;
903 p.

*B*ased on the 1967 movie starring Julie Andrews, *Thoroughly Modern Millie* is a new musical, retaining only three of the songs from the movie (including the title song), with a score by Jeanine Tesori. It chronicles the life of Millie, a transplanted Kansas girl trying to make it big in New York in the flapper days of the 1920s. She stays with other young starlets at the Hotel Priscilla, which is run by the sinister Mrs. Meers, who actually is running a white slave trade on the side. The madcap plot has many twists and turns, and shows a cheery slice of life in New York during the Jazz age. Millie decides in the end that it is only love she is interested in. With "Thoroughly Modern Millie," Millie announces her arrival and tells the world to "beat the drums, 'cause here comes thoroughly…modern Millie now."

HAIRSPRAY

Music:
Marc Shaiman

Lyrics:
Scott Wittman, Marc Shaiman,
based on the film written and directed by
John Waters

Book:
Mark O'Donnell, Thomas Meehan

Producers:
Margo Lion, Adam Epstein,
The Baruch-Viertel-Routh-Frankel Group, etc.

Director:
Jack O'Brien

Choreographer:
Jerry Mitchell

Cast:
Laura Bell Bundy, Kerry Butler,
Harvey Fierstein, Adam Fleming,
Jennifer Gambatese, Linda Hart, John Hill,

Dick Latessa, Matthew Morrison,
Corey Reynolds, Peter Matthew Smith,
Clarke Thorell, Danelle Eugenia Wilson,
Marossa Jaret Winokur

Songs:
Good Morning Baltimore
The Nicest Kids in Town
Mama, I'm a Big Girl Now
I Can Hear the Bells
It Takes Two
Welcome to the 60's
Run and Tell That
Big, Blonde and Beautiful
Timeless to Me
Without Love
I Know Where I've Been
Hairspray
You Can't Stop the Beat

New York Run:
Neil Simon Theatre, August 15, 2002;
still running April, 2006

*F*ilm composer Marc Shaiman helped turn John Waters' campy 1988 movie *Hairspray* into perfect fodder for a new Broadway musical—teenage angst, racial integration, a lot of dancing and a whole lot of hair. Plump heroine Tracy Turnblad dreams of dancing on the Corny Collins TV show, but is upstaged by the prettier, but less talented, current "It-girl" Amber Von Tussle. Tracy envisions good things for herself, as she knows she can take down Amber in "I Can Hear the Bells." Amber has the support of her overbearing mother, Velma, who is also the producer for Corny Collins. Velma, a former child star, waxes poetic on her fame, and rages that Tracy will never reach the heights Velma did when she was "Miss Baltimore Crabs." Tracy eventually dances her way onto the show and gains acceptance for all teens of every size, shape and color.

MOVIN' OUT

Music and Lyrics:
Billy Joel

Concept:
Twyla Tharp

Producers:
James L. Nederlander, Hal Luftig,
Scott E. Nederlander, etc.

Director:
Scott Wise

Choreographer:
Twyla Tharp

Cast:
Benjamin G. Bowman, Michael Cavanaugh,
Elizabeth Parkinson, Keith Roberts,
John Selya, Ashley Tuttle, Scott Wise

Songs:
Scenes from an Italian Restaurant
Movin' Out (Anthony's Song)
Reverie (Villa D'Este)

Just the Way You Are
The Longest Time
Uptown Girl
Summer, Highland Falls
Waltz #1 (Nunley's Carousel)
She's Got a Way
The Stranger
Invention #1 in C Minor
Big Shot
Big Man on Mulberry Street
Pressure
Goodnight Saigon
Shameless
The River of Dreams
Keeping the Faith
Only the Good Die Young
I've Loved These Days

New York Run:
Richard Rodgers Theatre, October 24, 2002;
1303 p.

*T*wyla Tharp had choreographed some Billy Joel songs for use in her dance studio, which gave rise to the idea of creating an entire show based around Joel's music. Receiving approval from the songwriter after sending him a videotape of her rehearsals, Tharp began to cull songs she could use to help frame a story. *Movin' Out* is that tale, completely danced, with no dialogue except the original lyrics of the songs. Joel himself picked out the players in the sound-alike, onstage band. The show chronicles the lives of a group of characters, from the naïve, we-can-do-it spirit of the 1950s, through the disenchantment of the Vietnam era, to the hope that all of them found later in life. In "Goodnight Saigon," a disenchanted veteran looks back on the camaraderie he felt in the Vietnam days.

AVENUE Q

Music and Lyrics:
Robert Lopez, Jeff Marx

Book:
Jeff Whitty

Producers:
Kevin McCollum, Robyn Goodman,
Jeffrey Seller, etc.

Director:
Jason Moore

Choreographer:
Ken Roberson

Cast:
Jennifer Barnhart, Natalie Venetia Belcon,
Stephanie D'Abruzzo, Jordan Gelber,
Ann Haraada, Rich Lyon, John Tartaglia

Songs:
The Avenue Q Theme
What Do You Do with a B.A. in English?
It Sucks to Be Me

If You Were Gay
Purpose
Everyone's a Little Bit Racist
The Internet Is for Porn
Mix Tape
I'm Not Wearing Underwear Today
Special
You Can Be as Loud as the Hell You Want
(When You're Makin' Love)
Fantasies Come True
My Girlfriend, Who Lives in Canada
There's a Fine, Fine Line
There Is Life Outside Your Apartment
The More You Ruv Someone
Schadenfreude
I Wish I Could Go Back to College
The Money Song
For Now

New York Run:
John Golden Theatre, July 31, 2003;
still running April, 2006

*A*venue Q is an ironic homage to "Sesame Street," though the puppet characters are much more adult, dealing with topics such as loud lovemaking, closeted homosexuality, and internet porn addiction. The puppeteers are onstage, acting and singing for their characters, but there are also humans in the production. The story deals with a young college graduate, Princeton, who learns how to live life and find love in New York. Along the way we meet the many tenants in his apartment building on Avenue Q. Princeton and his love interest Kate Monster hit some rocky times, and as they break up, Kate sadly muses "There's a Fine, Fine Line" between a lover and a friend.

THE BOY FROM OZ

Music and Lyrics:
Peter Allen

Book:
Martin Sherman

Producers:
Ben Gannon, Robert Fox

Director:
Philip William McKinley

Choreographer:
Joel McKneely

Cast:
Stephanie J. Block, Jarrod Emick,
Mitchel David Federan, Beth Fowler,
Hugh Jackman, Isabel Keating,
Michael Mulheren

Songs:
The Lives of Me
Arthur's Theme (Best That You Can Do)
Come Save Me
Quiet Please, There's a Lady on Stage
I'd Rather Leave While I'm in Love
Not the Boy Next Door
Bi-Coastal
If You Were Wondering
Everything Old Is New Again
Love Don't Need a Reason
I Honestly Love You
You and Me (We Wanted It All)
I Still Call Australia Home
Don't Cry Out Loud
I Go to Rio

New York Run:
Imperial Theatre, October 16, 2003;
364 p.

*A*ustralian-born Peter Allen was a quintessential 1970s performer, a rags to riches, Australian bush country to Radio City Music Hall story. This musical biography uses the songs that Allen wrote throughout his life, many of which were already autobiographical, to weave together the story of this flamboyant performer from meager beginnings, to marriage with Liza Minnelli, to his own death of AIDS. "Don't Cry Out Loud" appears late in the show, sung by Peter's mother Marion. This ballad shows Peter's compulsion to hide his feelings deep within himself, while putting forward a flashy, untouchable personality. Drawing on the success of the Sydney production, *The Boy from Oz* came to Broadway in 2003 as a star vehicle for another Aussie, movie star Hugh Jackman.

WICKED

Music and Lyrics:
Stephen Schwartz

Book:
Winnie Holzman,
based on the novel by Gregory Maguire

Producers:
Marc Platt, Universal Pictures, etc.

Director:
Joe Mantello

Choreographer:
Wayne Cilento

Cast:
Norbert Leo Butz, Kristin Chenoweth,
Michelle Federer, Christopher Fitzgerald,
Joel Grey, Idina Menzel,
Carole Shelley, William Youmans

Songs:
No One Mourns the Wicked
The Wizard and I
What Is This Feeling?
Dancing through Life
Popular
I'm Not That Girl
One Short Day
Defying Gravity
Thank Goodness
Wonderful
As Long as You're Mine
No Good Deed
For Good

New York Run:
George Gershwin Theatre, October 30, 2003;
still running April, 2006

*S*tephen Schwartz's return to Broadway came with *the* hit of 2003, *Wicked*. Based on Gregory Maguire's 1995 book, the musical chronicles the backstory of the Wicked Witch of the West, Elphaba, and Good Witch of the North, Glinda (Galinda), before their story threads are picked up in L. Frank Baum's *The Wonderful Wizard of Oz*. At times a dark show, the original production was characterized by lavish sets and a stellar cast, including Kristin Chenoweth, Idina Menzel, Norbert Leo Butz, and Broadway immortal Joel Grey. The two witches first cross paths back in school as unlikely roommates. Elphaba, shy and green, learns from radiant Galinda just what it takes to be "Popular."

DIRTY ROTTEN SCOUNDRELS

Music and Lyrics:
David Yazbek

Book:
Jeffrey Lane

Producers:
Marty Bell, David Brown, Aldo Scrofani, etc.

Director:
Jack O'Brien

Choreographer:
Jerry Mitchell

Cast:
Norbert Leo Butz, John Lithgow,
Sara Gettelfinger, Joanna Gleason,
Gregory Jbara, Sherie Rene Scott

Songs:
Give Them What They Want
What Was a Woman to Do
Great Big Stuff
Chimp in a Suit
Oklahoma?
All About Ruprecht
Here I Am
Nothing Is Too Wonderful to Be True
Rüffhousin' mit Shüffhausen
Like Zis/Like Zat
The More We Dance
Love Is My Legs
Love Sneaks In
Son of Great Big Stuff
The Reckoning

New York Run:
Imperial Theatre, March 3, 2005;
still running April, 2006

*D*avid Yazbek's follow-up to *The Full Monty* (2000) was again based on a movie. *Dirty Rotten Scoundrels* takes its name and plot from the 1988 movie starring Michael Caine and Steve Martin, which itself was a remake of the 1964 movie *Bedtime Story*, starring David Niven, Marlon Brando and Shirley Jones. The essential story remains the same. Two con men are initially at their game separately, preying upon wealthy women of the French Riviera. The suave, British Lawrence Jameson (John Lithgow) wines and dines women out of their money, posing as a rich, deposed prince. Crass American Freddy Benson (Norbert Leo Butz) tries to usurp the female fortune through a sob story. When the two grifters meet, they decide that the French Riviera isn't big enough for both of them. They choose a mark, young heiress Christine Colgate (Sherie Rene Scott). Whoever gets to her money first will get to remain in town. In the end, after many double-crosses, the two scoundrels learn that they're not the only schemers on the French Riviera. Early on, eyes opened by the lavish lifestyle of the more successful Lawrence, Freddy realizes that he too wants "Great Big Stuff."

MONTY PYTHON'S SPAMALOT

Music:
John Du Prez, Eric Idle

Lyrics:
Eric Idle,
based on the screenplay *Monty Python and the Holy Grail* by Eric Idle, John Cleese, Terry Gilliam, Terry Jones, Michael Palin, Graham Chapman

Book:
Eric Idle

Producer:
Boyett Ostar Productions,
The Shubert Organization, etc.

Director:
Mike Nichols

Choreographer:
Casey Nicholaw

Cast:
Hank Azaria, Christian Borle, Tim Curry,
Michael McGrath, David Hyde Pierce,

Sara Ramirez, Steve Rosen,
Christopher Sieber

Songs:
Finland/Fisch Schlapping Dance
Monks Chant / He Is Not Dead Yet
Come with Me
Laker Girls Cheer
The Song That Goes Like This
All for One
Knights of the Round Table
Find Your Grail
Run Away!
Always Look on the Bright Side of Life
Brave Sir Robin
You Won't Succeed on Broadway
What Ever Happened to My Part?
Where Are You?
His Name Is Lancelot
I'm All Alone

New York Run:
Shubert Theatre, March 17, 2005;
still running April, 2006

*E*ric Idle, one of the founding members of the British television comedy troupe "Monty Python's Flying Circus," made his Broadway writing debut with *Monty Python's Spamalot*, billed as "a new musical lovingly ripped off from the motion picture *Monty Python and the Holy Grail*." As in the movie, the show involves the wacky adventures of King Arthur and his band of knights in their search for the Holy Grail, shrubbery, and in the musical, success on the Great White Way. The lavish *Spamalot* was directed by luminary Broadway and movie director Mike Nichols. The original cast starred Tim Curry, Hank Azaria and David Hyde Pierce. True to characteristic Python irreverence and silliness, *Spamalot* lambastes the musical genre at every step, one such example being the aptly named "The Song That Goes Like This," sung by The Lady of the Lake and Sir Dennis Galahad.

THE LIGHT IN THE PIAZZA

Music and Lyrics:
Adam Guettel

Book:
Craig Lucas,
based on the novel by Elizabeth Spencer

Producers:
Lincoln Center Theater, LCT Musical Theater,
by arrangement with
Turner Entertainment Co.

Director:
Bartlett Sher

Choreographer:
Jonathan Butterell

Cast:
Michael Berresse, Sarah Uriarte Berry,
Victoria Clark, Patti Cohenour, Beau Gravitte,
Mark Harelik, Matthew Morrison,
Kelli O'Hara

Songs:
Statues and Stories
The Beauty Is
Il mondo era vuoto
Passeggiata
Dividing Day
Say It Somehow
The Light in the Piazza
Let's Walk
Love to Me
Fable

New York Run:
Vivian Beaumont Theatre, April 18, 2005;
still running April, 2006

*F*inding inspiration in the same country as his grandfather Richard Rodgers' *Do I Hear a Waltz?*, Adam Guettel's *The Light in the Piazza* follows Americans abroad in Italy. The plot concerns a mother and her daughter Clara on extended holiday in Florence in 1953. Clara is mentally challenged, having the mind of a ten-year-old, but the passions of a young woman. An Italian man, Fabrizio, falls for the beautiful girl, and much of the story revolves around Clara's mother trying to protect her child from a perceived incompatibility with the young suitor. Overhearing her mother discussing with her father Clara's upcoming marriage, Clara becomes upset and runs to break it off with Fabrizio. He comforts her in "Love to Me." In the end, Clara and Fabrizio will be married. A non-musical movie treatment was made in 1962, starring Olivia de Havilland and Rossano Brazzi.

I WANT TO GO TO HOLLYWOOD

from the Broadway Musical GRAND HOTEL

Words and Music by
MAURY YESTON

Parlando

What did he see in me? What's my at-trac-tion? Could

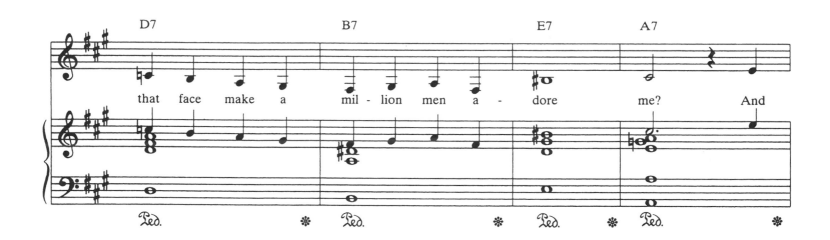

that face make a mil-lion men a - dore me? And

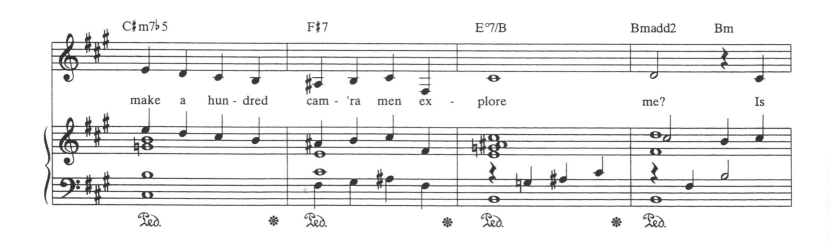

make a hun-dred cam-'ra men ex - plore me? Is

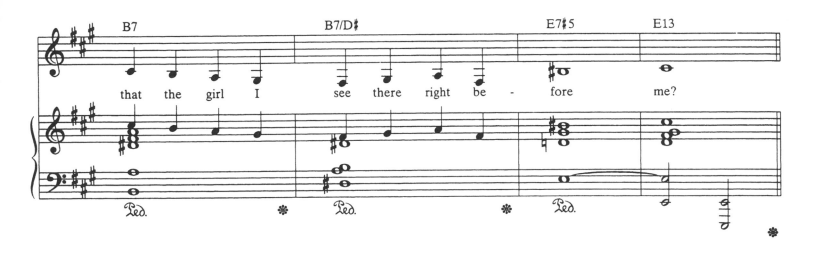

With a swing ♩ = 92

I wan - na be that girl in the mir - ror there. I wan - na be that

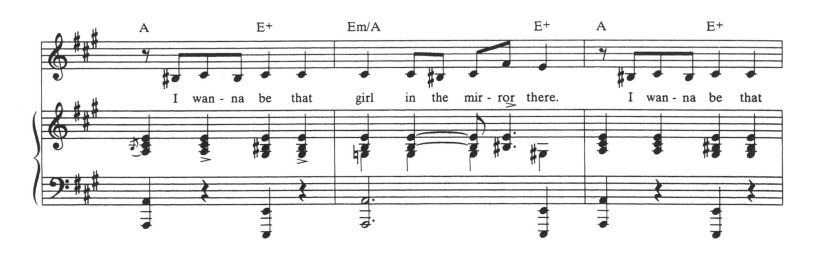

girl with gold - en hair. Up on a sil - ver screen,____ most ev - 'ry - where

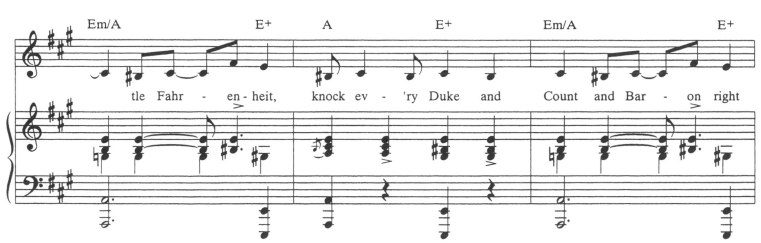

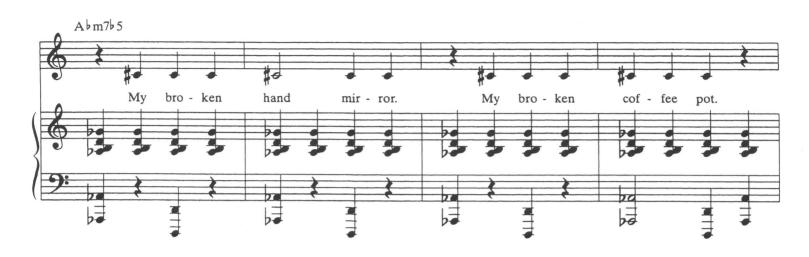

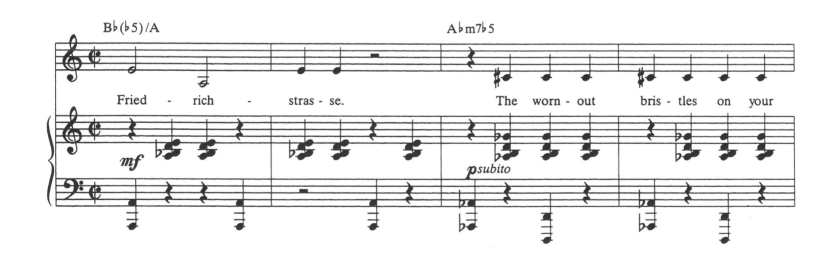

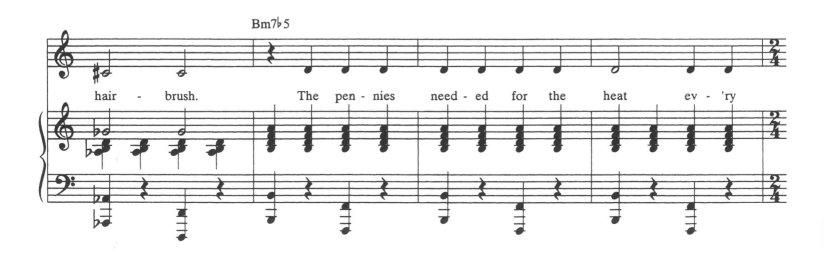

24

LOVE CHANGES EVERYTHING

from ASPECTS OF LOVE

Music by ANDREW LLOYD WEBBER
Lyrics by DON BLACK and CHARLES HART

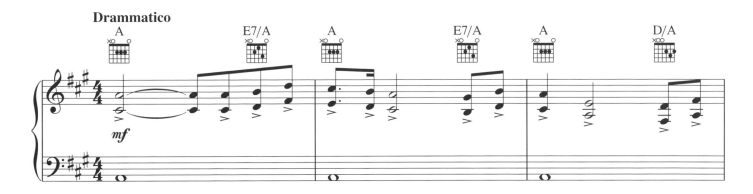

Love, love chang-es ev-'ry-thing: hands and
Love, love chang-es ev-'ry-thing: days are

fac-es, earth and sky. Love, love chang-es
long-er, words mean more. Love, can break the

28

I'D GIVE MY LIFE FOR YOU

from MISS SAIGON

Music by CLAUDE-MICHEL SCHÖNBERG
Lyrics by RICHARD MALTBY JR. and ALAIN BOUBLIL
Adapted from original French Lyrics by ALAIN BOUBLIL

BEAUTY AND THE BEAST

from Walt Disney's BEAUTY AND THE BEAST: THE BROADWAY MUSICAL

Lyrics by HOWARD ASHMAN
Music by ALAN MENKEN

40

WITH ONE LOOK

from SUNSET BOULEVARD

Music by ANDREW LLOYD WEBBER
Lyrics by DON BLACK and CHRISTOPHER HAMPTON,
with contributions by AMY POWERS

NORMA:

With one look I can break your heart, with one look I play ev-ery part. I can make your sad heart sing, with one look you'll know all you need to know. With one smile I'm the girl next door

LIVING IN THE SHADOWS

from VICTOR/VICTORIA

Words by LESLIE BRICUSSE
Music by FRANK WILDHORN

Moderately slow

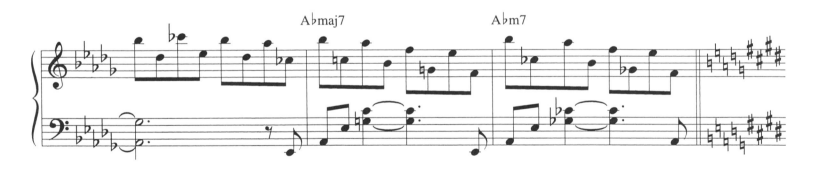

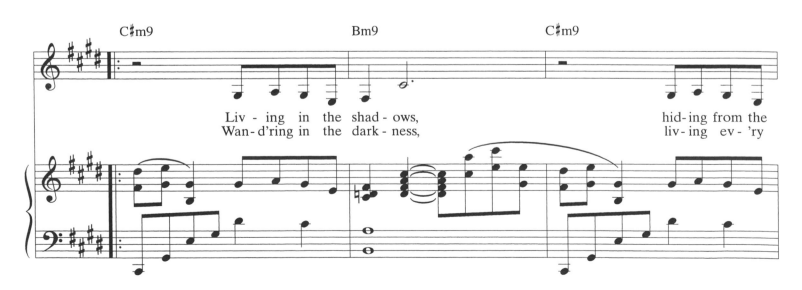

Liv - ing in the shad - ows,
Wan - d'ring in the dark - ness,

hid - ing from the
liv - ing ev - 'ry

48

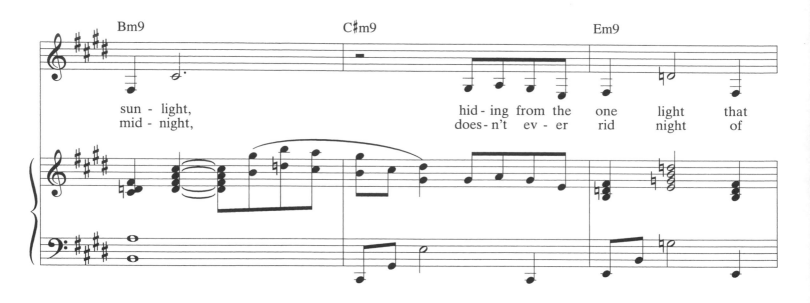

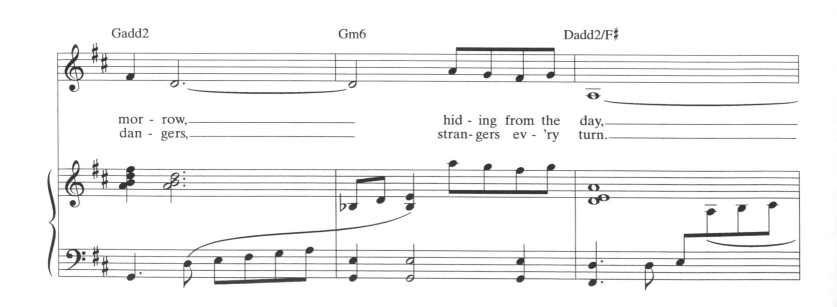

SEASONS OF LOVE

from RENT

Words and Music by
JONATHAN LARSON

56

THIS IS THE MOMENT

from JEKYLL & HYDE

Words by LESLIE BRICUSSE
Music by FRANK WILDHORN

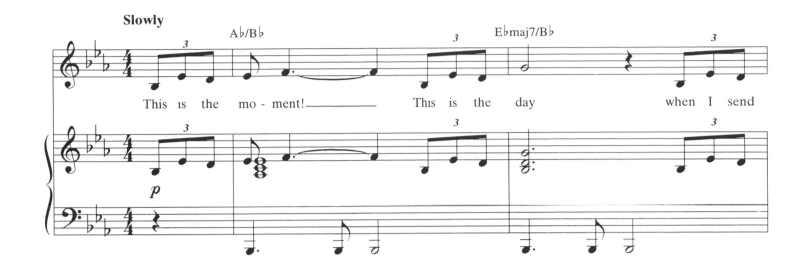

GODSPEED TITANIC
(Sail On)
from TITANIC

Music and Lyrics by
MAURY YESTON

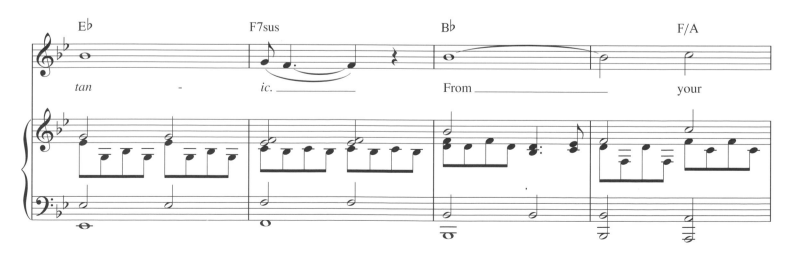

WHO WILL LOVE ME AS I AM?

from SIDE SHOW

Words by BILL RUSSELL
Music by HENRY KRIEGER

Daisy and Violet sing this number as a duet in the show; adapted as a solo for this edition.

*optional duet part

THEY LIVE IN YOU

Disney Presents THE LION KING: THE BROADWAY MUSICAL

Music and Lyrics by MARK MANCINA,
JAY RIFKIN and LEBO M

76

ELABORATE LIVES

from Elton John and Tim Rice's AIDA

Music by ELTON JOHN
Lyrics by TIM RICE

80

LET IT GO
from THE FULL MONTY

Words and Music by
DAVID YAZBEK

SPRINGTIME FOR HITLER

from THE PRODUCERS

Music and Lyrics by
MEL BROOKS

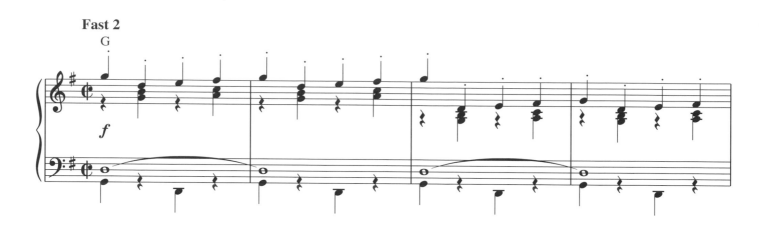

Ger - ma - ny was hav - ing trou - ble, what a sad, sad sto - ry,

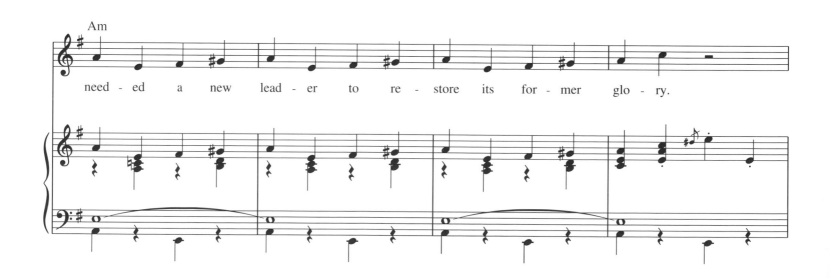

need - ed a new lead - er to re - store its for - mer glo - ry.

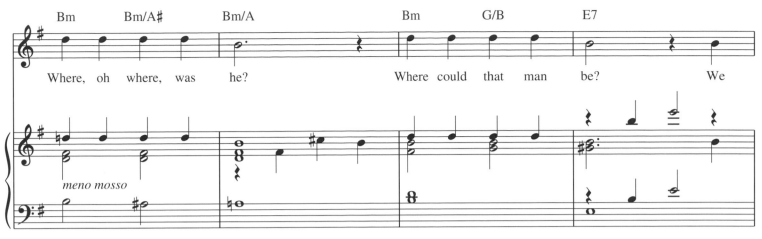

CHORUS:

Spring - time for Hit - ler and Ger - ma - ny, (spring - time, spring - time,

spring-time, spring-time, spring-time, spring-time spring-time!_) Come on

Swing, molto accel.

Ger - mans, go in - to your dance!

FOLLOW YOUR HEART

from URINETOWN

Music and Lyrics by MARK HOLLMANN
Book and Lyrics by GREG KOTIS

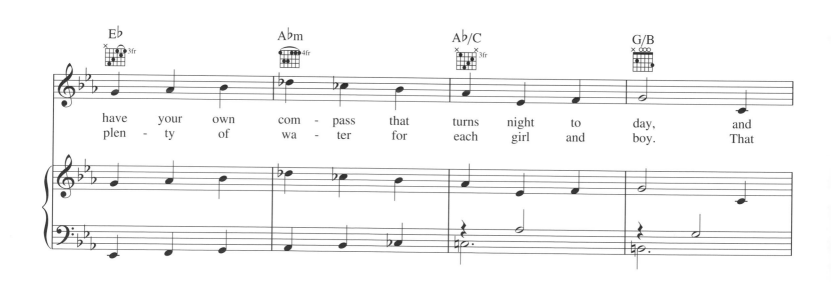

112

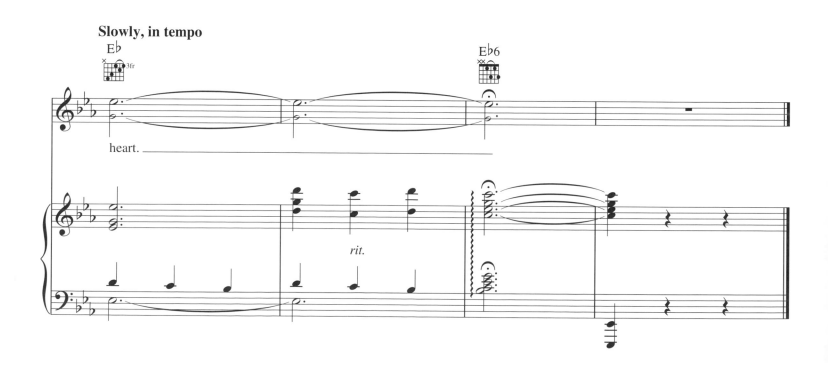

DANCING QUEEN

from MAMMA MIA!

Words and Music by BENNY ANDERSSON,
BJÖRN ULVAEUS and STIG ANDERSON

THOROUGHLY MODERN MILLIE

from THOROUGHLY MODERN MILLIE

Words by SAMMY CAHN
Music by JAMES VAN HEUSEN

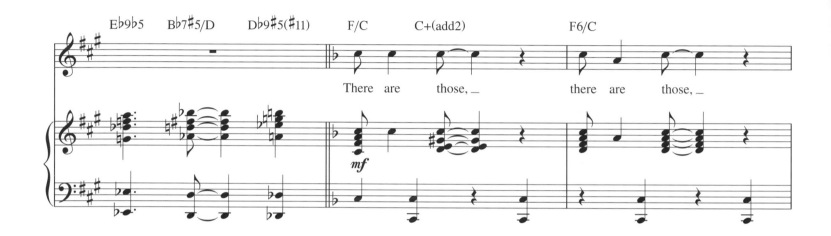

heav - en knows, _ the world has gone to rack _ and to ruin.

What we think is chic, u - nique, and quite a - dor - a - ble, _

I CAN HEAR THE BELLS

from HAIRSPRAY

Music by MARC SHAIMAN
Lyrics by MARC SHAIMAN and SCOTT WITTMAN

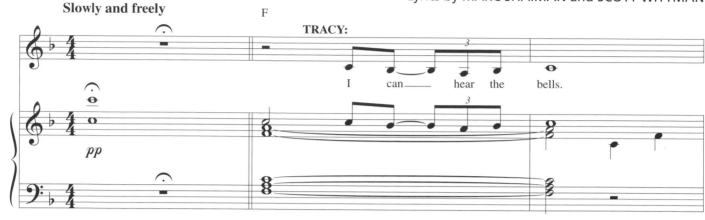

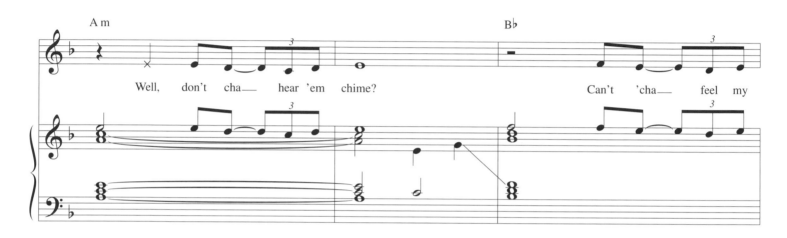

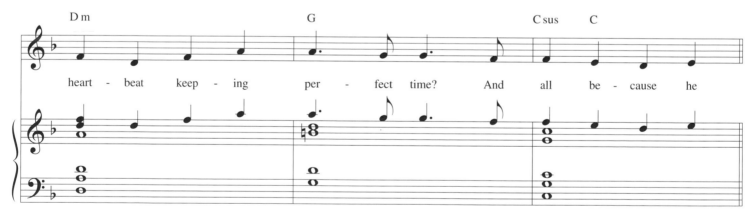

GOODNIGHT SAIGON
from MOVIN' OUT

Words and Music by
BILLY JOEL

Slow and steady

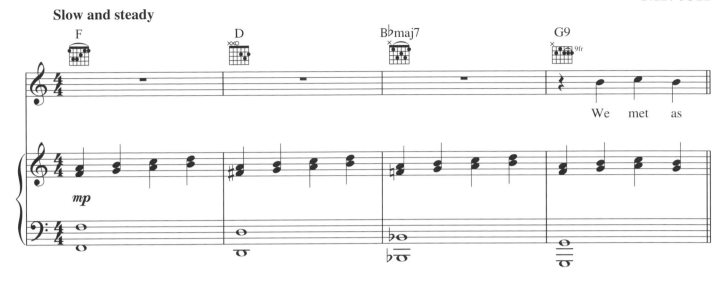

We met as

soul mates / On Par - is / Is - land / We left as / in - mates / From an a -
spas - tic / like tame - less / hors - es / We left in / plas - tic / As num - bered

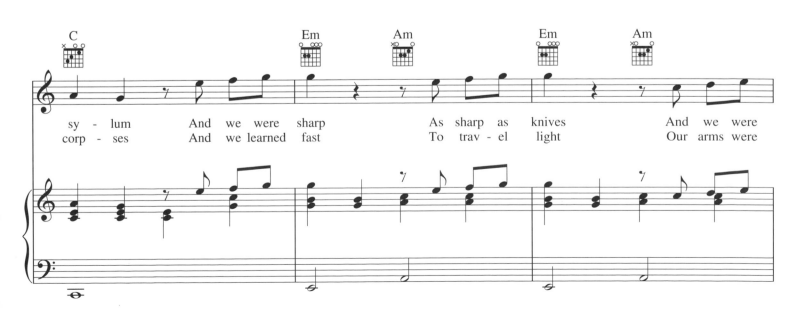

sy - lum / And we were sharp / As sharp as / knives / And we were
corp - ses / And we learned fast / To trav - el / light / Our arms were

140

142

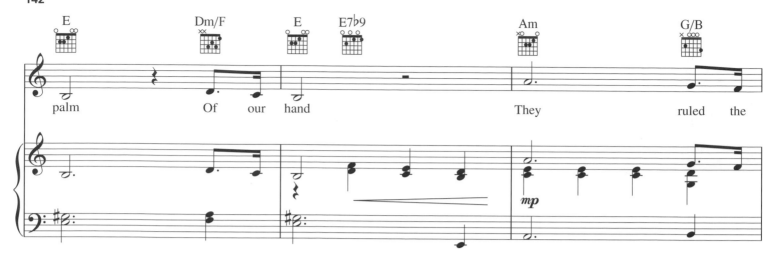

D.S. al Coda

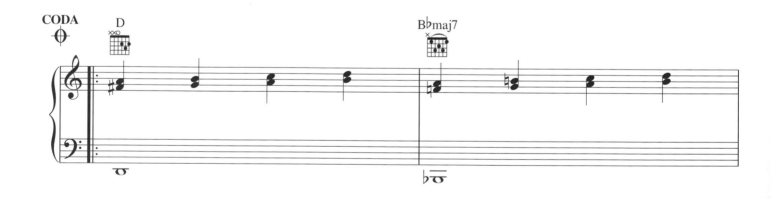

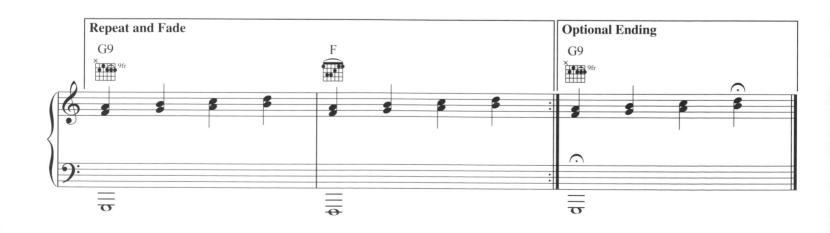

THERE'S A FINE, FINE LINE

from AVENUE Q

Music and Lyrics by ROBERT LOPEZ
and JEFF MARX

Moderate Folk Rock

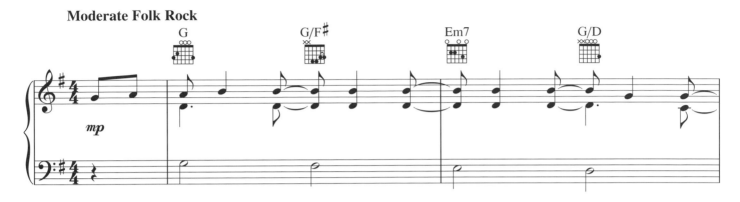

KATE:

There's a fine, fine line ___

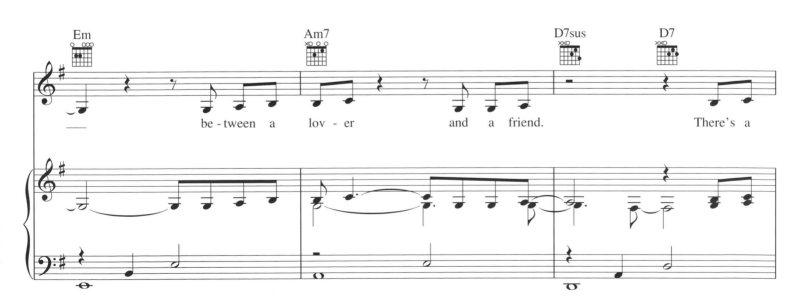

be - tween a lov - er and a friend. There's a

There's a

fine, fine line _____ be - tween love _____

and a waste _ of ___ time. _____

DON'T CRY OUT LOUD
(We Don't Cry Out Loud)
from THE BOY FROM OZ

Words and Music by PETER ALLEN
and CAROLE BAYER SAGER

Don't cry __ out loud, _____ just keep it in - side, learn how to
Fly high __ and proud, _____ and if you should fall re - mem - ber you

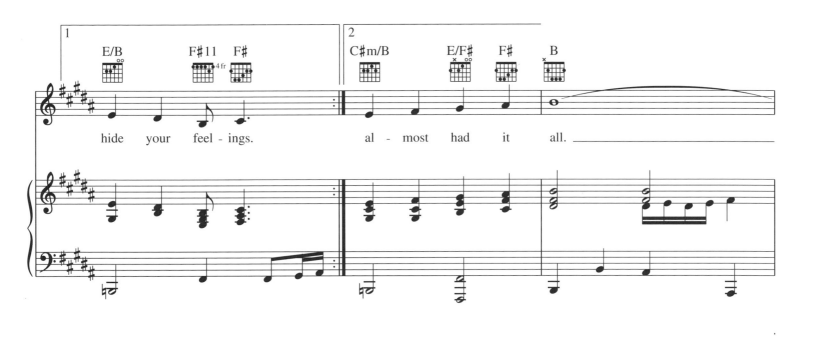

hide your feel - ings. al - most had it all. _____

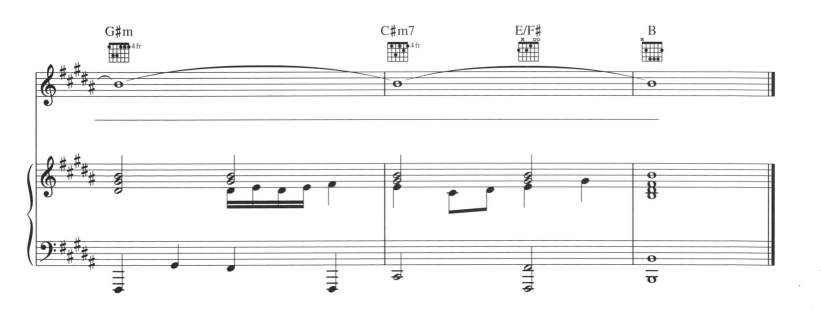

POPULAR
from WICKED

Music and Lyrics by
STEPHEN SCHWARTZ

Sweetly

When-ev-er I see some-one less for-tu-nate than I— and let's

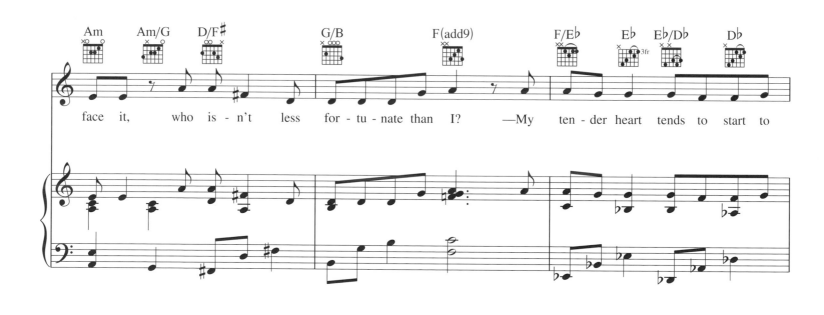

face it, who is-n't less for-tu-nate than I? —My ten-der heart tends to start to

bleed   And when some-one needs a make-o-ver, I sim-ply have to take o-ver; I

GREAT BIG STUFF

from DIRTY ROTTEN SCOUNDRELS

Words and Music by
DAVID YAZBEK

What do I want?   *I want this!*

I want ... this!   *I want ... this!*   (vulgarly)   I thought I

had a re - al gift, the pen - ny an - te grift, but, Fred-dy's get - tin' read - y now to

give his life a lift. I'm tired of be-in' a chump. I wan - na be like Trump. Two

o-ne on the phone, he's got a par-ty go-ing on. And Hef 'll have me o-ver to

play some na-ked Twist-er, blot-to in the grot-to with a play-mate and her sis-ter!

ENSEMBLE:
Great big stuff!

FREDDY: *Rap stars'll love me!*

ENSEMBLE:
Great big stuff!

FREDDY: *Get me a posse! A'ight?*

ENSEMBLE:
Great big stuff!

FREDDY:
Chill-in' in the cit-y, sit-tin'

THE SONG THAT GOES LIKE THIS

from MONTY PYTHON'S SPAMALOT

Lyrics by ERIC IDLE
Music by JOHN DU PREZ and ERIC IDLE

Moderately, but with great intensity

DENNIS: Once, ____ in ev'ry show there comes a song like this. It starts off ___ soft and low, and ends up ___ with a kiss. Oh, where is the song that goes like this?

LOVE TO ME
from THE LIGHT IN THE PIAZZA

Words and Music by
ADAM GUETTEL

Tenderly

FABRIZIO:

The day we meet, the way you lean a - gainst the wind and do not

no - tice how you hun - ger for sur - prise,

and do not think that you are tall e-nough,

like you're stand - ing on_____ a

moun - tain-side_____ a - lone._____ This is what I

just so I can be there. This is how I know.

This is what I see. This is love to

me.

Rit.

HAL LEONARD:
Your Source for the Best of Broadway

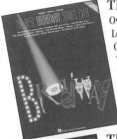

THE BEST BROADWAY SONGS EVER
Over 70 songs from Broadway's latest and greatest hit shows: As Long as He Needs Me • Bess, You Is My Woman • Bewitched • Comedy Tonight • Don't Cry for Me Argentina • Getting to Know You • I Could Have Danced All Night • I Dreamed a Dream • If I Were a Rich Man • The Last Night of the World • Love Changes Everything • Oklahoma • Ol' Man River • People • Try to Remember • and more.
00309155 Piano/Vocal/Guitar....................$22.95

THE BIG BOOK OF BROADWAY
This edition includes 70 songs from classic musicals and recent blockbusters like *The Producers, Aida* and *Hairspray*. Includes: Bring Him Home • Camelot • Everything's Coming Up Roses • The Impossible Dream • A Lot of Livin' to Do • One • Some Enchanted Evening • Thoroughly Modern Millie • Till There Was You • and more.
00311658 Piano/Vocal/Guitar $19.95

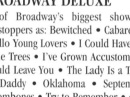

BROADWAY CLASSICS
PIANO PLAY-ALONG SERIES, VOLUME 4
This book/CD pack provides keyboardists with a full performance track and a separate backing track for each tune. Songs include: Ain't Misbehavin' • Cabaret • If I Were a Bell • Memory • Oklahoma • Some Enchanted Evening • The Sound of Music • You'll Never Walk Alone.
00311075 Book/CD Pack $12.95

BROADWAY DELUXE
125 of Broadway's biggest show tunes! Includes such showstoppers as: Bewitched • Cabaret • Camelot • Day by Day • Hello Young Lovers • I Could Have Danced All Night • I Talk to the Trees • I've Grown Accustomed to Her Face • If Ever I Would Leave You • The Lady Is a Tramp • My Heart Belongs to Daddy • Oklahoma • September Song • Seventy Six Trombones • Try to Remember • and more!
00309245 Piano/Vocal/Guitar $24.95

BROADWAY SONGS
Get more bang for your buck with this jam-packed collection of 73 songs from 56 shows, including *Annie Get Your Gun, Cabaret, The Full Monty, Jekyll & Hyde, Les Misérables, Oklahoma* and more. Songs: Any Dream Will Do • Consider Yourself • Footloose • Getting to Know You • I Dreamed a Dream • One • People • Summer Nights • The Surrey with the Fringe on Top • With One Look • and more.
00310832 Piano/Vocal/Guitar..................$12.95

CONTEMPORARY BROADWAY
44 songs from 25 contemporary musicals and Broadway revivals. Includes: And All That Jazz (*Chicago*) • Dancing Queen (*Mamma Mia!*) • Good Morning Baltimore (*Hairspray*) • Mein Herr (*Cabaret*) • Popular (*Wicked*) • Purpose (*Avenue Q*) • Seasons of Love (*Rent*) • When You Got It, Flaunt It (*The Producers*) • You Rule My World (*The Full Monty*) • and more.
00310796 Piano/Vocal/Guitar..................$18.95

DEFINITIVE BROADWAY
142 of the greatest show tunes ever, including: Don't Cry for Me Argentina • Hello, Dolly! • I Dreamed a Dream • Lullaby of Broadway • Mack the Knife • Memory • Send in the Clowns • Somewhere • The Sound of Music • Strike Up the Band • Summertime • Sunrise, Sunset • Tea for Two • Tomorrow • What I Did for Love • and more.
00359570 Piano/Vocal/Guitar..................$24.95

ESSENTIAL SONGS: BROADWAY
Over 100 songs are included in this top-notch collection: Any Dream Will Do • Blue Skies • Cabaret • Don't Cry for Me, Argentina • Edelweiss • Hello, Dolly! • I'll Be Seeing You • Memory • The Music of the Night • Oklahoma • Seasons of Love • Summer Nights • There's No Business like Show Business • Tomorrow • and more.
00311222 Piano/Vocal/Guitar $24.95

KIDS' BROADWAY SONGBOOK
An unprecedented collection of songs originally performed by children on the Broadway stage. Includes 16 songs for boys and girls, including: Gary, Indiana (*The Music Man*) • Castle on a Cloud (*Les Misérables*) • Where Is Love? (*Oliver!*) • Tomorrow (*Annie*) • and more.
00311609 Book Only.......................$12.95
00740149 Book/CD Pack.................$19.95

THE OFF-BROADWAY SONGBOOK
42 gems from off-Broadway hits, including *Godspell, Tick Tick...Boom!, The Fantasticks, Once upon a Mattress, The Wild Party* and more. Songs include: Always a Bridesmaid • Come to Your Senses • Day by Day • Happiness • How Glory Goes • I Hate Musicals • The Picture in the Hall • Soon It's Gonna Rain • Stars and the Moon • Still Hurting • Twilight • and more.
00311168 Piano/Vocal/Guitar $16.95

THE TONY AWARDS SONGBOOK
This collection assembles songs from 56 years of Tony-winning musicals selected for their "singability and joy." Songs include: Til There Was You • The Sound of Music • Hello, Dolly! • Sunrise, Sunset • Send in the Clowns • Tomorrow • Memory • I Dreamed a Dream • Seasons of Love • Circle of Life • Mama, I'm a Big Girl Now • and more. Includes photos and a table of contents listed both chronologically and alphabetically.
00311092 Piano/Vocal/Guitar $19.95

THE ULTIMATE BROADWAY FAKE BOOK
Over 700 songs from more than 200 Broadway shows! Songs include: All I Ask of You • Bewitched • Cabaret • Don't Cry for Me Argentina • Edelweiss • Getting to Know You • Hello, Dolly! • If I Were a Rich Man • Last Night of the World • The Music of the Night • Oklahoma • People • Seasons of Love • Tell Me on a Sunday • Unexpected Song • and more!
00240046 Melody/Lyrics/Chords.....................$45.00

ULTIMATE BROADWAY PLATINUM
100 popular Broadway songs: As If We Never Said Goodbye • Bye Bye Birdie • Camelot • Everything's Coming Up Roses • Gigi • Hello, Young Lovers • I Enjoy Being a Girl • Just in Time • My Favorite Things • On a Clear Day • People • Sun and Moon • Try to Remember • Who Can I Turn To • Younger Than Springtime • and many more.
00311496 Piano/Vocal/Guitar $19.95

Prices, contents, and availability subject to change without notice.
Some products may not be available outside the U.S.A.

FOR MORE INFORMATION, SEE YOUR LOCAL MUSIC DEALER,
OR WRITE TO:

HAL•LEONARD®
CORPORATION
7777 W. BLUEMOUND RD. P.O. BOX 13819 MILWAUKEE, WI 53213

Get complete songlists and more at www.halleonard.com

0306